AFTER CURFEW

Julie Bloss Kelsey

After Curfew

©2023 Julie Bloss Kelsey
All Rights Reserved

First Printing

ISBN 978-1-7350257-5-9

CUTTLEFISH BOOKS

AFTER CURFEW

*This collection is dedicated
to the memory
of my awkward adolescent self
and to those who see themselves
reflected on these pages.*

roller rink birthday—
my friends pay a boy
to skate with me

too-high heels
learning to walk
the second time

following her
out the window
my judgment

after curfew
ducking each time
we see headlights

crammed into
some teen's car
a bottle of whiskey

cruising for boys
no idea what to do
if we catch one

not quite ready
to be called my boyfriend
my boy friend

don't tell anyone
he hands me
a valentine

passing notes
in the old town library—
our first date

finally fitting in—
your school ID
in my wallet

sneaking out
to meet at the movies
popcorn kisses

inviting him over
when my parents aren't home
first hickey

just hold me, he says
riding without
a helmet

creased yearbook page
where you wrote
love

cradling you
until we both fall asleep
midnight phone calls

I worry he loves her
more than me . . .
black Camaro

leather and lace . . .
the other girls' baby pink
prom dresses

after the dance
he detours up a canyon . . .
topless in the back seat

mood music
from the car stereo . . .
Ozzy Osbourne

make-out session
he screws in
his colored light bulb

the last
of the ice cream
spooning

third base—
I buy a pregnancy test
just in case

showering with a boy
where to put
my hands

seeing him
with another girl . . .
cigarettes and karaoke

mixing everything
in the liquor cabinet
first time drunk

strangers at the bar
trying to remember
my fake name

he says he's famous
in the minor league
sports bar

knowing it's a bad idea
and doing it anyway . . .
beer pressure

face-first
in a stranger's lap
tequila shots

intoxicated
she pulls me up
by my hair

still thankful
I didn't taste it—
moonshine

buzzed
in the back of a pickup
endless stars

sobering up
I tell everyone
I'm a virgin

confessing my sins
the priest presses me
for details

goody two-shoes
no one suspects
a thing

AUTHOR'S NOTE

This poetry collection began at an online launch party for Rowan Beckett's chapbook, *Hot Girl Haiku* (Cuttlefish Books). As part of the games, participants were invited to write their own "hot girl haiku." I tried, but my haiku deviated from "hot" straight into "awkward." And yet, once I started writing about my gawky teens and early twenties, I couldn't seem to stop. My thanks to Rowan Beckett for the inspiration.

AFTERWORD

Adolescence and early adulthood is a time in life when we begin breaking away from the expectations of our parents and society. We spend years switching between conformity and anarchy until we finally gravitate towards whatever or whoever makes us most comfortable. However, you don't necessarily have to want popularity to desire or seek acceptance. We've all seen movies like *The Breakfast Club* and *Mean Girls*, and although they're dramatized for entertainment, the situations these kids find themselves in aren't far from reality.

Some scars might run deep, but puppy love, first heartbreaks, and "typical guy" problems are only surface level when it comes to the very real issues fem-presenting teens face. Unstable sense of self is one of the most detrimental experiences because it leaves us feeling alienated, and yet many young people ask themselves "Who am I? Where do I fit in?" Sometimes you have to lose yourself to figure out how to love yourself, but the results of this pressure can also include eating disorders, addiction, and depression. Other times, we can get through high school and college with very little bumps and bruises, even with parties every weekend. Either way, this (unfortunate) right of passage seems to be a hazing ritual into womanhood.

In 2019, Megan Thee Stallion challenged this perspective and instilled in us a new confidence by giving everyone permission to be a "hot girl" no matter who we are, what we look like, or where we come from. This internet phenomenon would become an entire movement for not just body positivity, but an entire cultural attitude. In my personal journey to elevate confessional poetry, I felt the need to integrate the Millennial experience into traditional haiku and senryu. My collection *Hot Girl Haiku* was inspired by Megan's idea to be "authentically YOU" and shares intimate moments, both loud and quiet, that showcase my voyage into a self-assured adult, plus all the mistakes I made getting there.

In these pages, Julie Bloss Kelsey takes us on her own evolutionary journey as we get to witness her transformation from this cute, awkward little duckling into a beautiful, confident black swan. Many of these moments might be "sugar, spice, and everything nice", but I find myself getting lost in every teenage dream I remember having. Even if individual experiences are unique and vary from person to person, this classic coming-of-age story is one every generation will be able to connect with.

Rowan Beckett
June 21, 2023

ABOUT THE AUTHOR

Julie Bloss Kelsey is a suburban mom who writes short-form poetry in her car as she shuttles her children to various events, often with an iced decaf latte in hand. She started writing haiku after the birth of her third child in 2009. Her first poetry collection, *The Call of Wildflowers*, is about motherhood. You can read it for free online through Moth Orchid Press (formerly Title IX Press). Connect with Julie on Instagram (@JulieBlossKelsey).

www.ingramcontent.com/pod-product-compliance
Lightning Source LLC
Chambersburg PA
CBHW061742070526
44585CB00024B/2773